2014
THE **JAMES BACKHOUSE** LECTURE

'Our life is love, and peace, and tenderness'

Bringing children into the centre of Quaker life and worship

TRACY BOURNE

THE JAMES BACKHOUSE LECTURES

The lectures were instituted by Australia Yearly Meeting of the Religious Society of Friends (Quakers) on its establishment in 1964.

They are named after James Backhouse who, with his companion, George Washington Walker, visited Australia from 1832 to 1838. They travelled widely, but spent most of their time in Tasmania. It was through their visit that Quaker Meetings were first established in Australia.

Coming to Australia under a concern for the conditions of convicts, the two men had access to people with authority in the young colonies, and with influence in Britain, both in Parliament and in the social reform movement. In meticulous reports and personal letters, they made practical suggestions and urged legislative action on penal reform, on the rum trade, and on land rights and the treatment of Aborigines.

James Backhouse was a general naturalist and a botanist. He made careful observations and published full accounts of what he saw, in addition to encouraging Friends in the colonies and following the deep concern that had brought him to Australia.

Australian Friends hope that this series of Lectures will bring fresh insights into the Truth, and speak to the needs and aspirations of Australian Quakerism. The present lecture was delivered at the Multi-Faith Centre, Griffith University, Nathan Campus, Brisbane, in January 2014.

Julian Robertson
Presiding Clerk
Australia Yearly Meeting

Front cover: Children inside a house they built together at Silver Wattle Quaker Centre. Photo by Tracy Bourne.

© The Religious Society of Friends (Quakers) in Australia, 2014

ISBN 978-0-9923857-0-5

Produced by Australia Yearly Meeting of the Religious Society of Friends (Quakers) in Australia Incorporated
Download copies from www.quakers.org.au or order from sales@quakers.org.au

Quakers
AUSTRALIA

Contents

About the author

Tracy Bourne is a member of Victoria Regional Meeting along with her husband Andrew Bray and three children, Emily, Rose and Miles Bray. As a child, she attended Catholic schools and was impressed by the dedication to social justice and religious mystery of the Sisters of Mercy. She and her family began attending Quaker meetings in 2003 after watching the ABC *Compass* program: *Seeking the Light Within*. She is a singer, singing teacher, theatre maker, and writer with an interest in new work that responds to the environment or to social justice issues. She lives in Ballarat, Victoria.

Acknowledgements

Thank you to Helen Bayes and Andrew Bray, who have offered editorial advice, personal support and spiritual direction over the course of preparing and writing this lecture.

The AYM Children and JYF Committee has inspired and supported this leading over the past few years; as have the many, many individual Friends who have offered wisdom and leadership on the ways that we can nurture children in our Society.

A very big thank you to the children and young people I have met and worshipped with over the past 10 years who have inspired me and taught me about the spirituality of play.

Finally, I want to thank my beautiful children and husband who have sustained me during the past year. Our life together is the substance of this leading.

Dedication

For Tony
26 February 2005

For the children who are no longer with us:
you live on in our hearts and in everything we do.

Foreword

Friends,

Our life is love, and peace, and tenderness; and bearing one with another, and forgiving one another, and not laying accusations one against another; but praying one for another, and helping one another up with a tender hand, if there has been any slip or fall; and waiting till the Lord gives sense and repentance, if sense and repentance in any be wanting.

Isaac Penington, 1667

Isaac Penington's letter to Amersham Friends Meeting has moved and upheld me as I've written this lecture. He is writing to a group that shares an uncertain and dangerous future: a group of Quakers who sought comfort in shared worship, and in simple communal rituals. His letter asks them to love and nurture each other, especially in moments of failure.

These early Friends placed themselves at great personal risks for the sake of Justice and Truth because they understood that their lives did not belong to them; they belonged to God. When they listened, they heard God ask for surprising things that were difficult and sometimes frightening. For them, living up to the Light was not about comfort and peace; it was about opening themselves up to the 'Refiner's Fire' that stripped them naked, so that they were unable to hide behind wealth, reputation, or anything of worldly value. Only the pure, unimpeded Light mattered.

As I have gone through the process of writing this lecture, I too have felt the 'Refiner's Fire' strip away my toughness. I have often felt raw, exposed, and vulnerable. I have had to face up to the weaknesses that are part of who I am. This isn't a comfortable place, but in a strange way I have felt liberated because I have come to understand that I can only write this lecture because I am imperfect.

In this lecture, I am asking Friends to open up to doubts about the ways that we live and worship. I am asking for big changes: There will be things to lay down, things to take on, and some uncertainty as we discern the right actions. It will be a time for us to listen well; to God, and to each other, as we bear each other up with a loving, tender hand.

All-age meeting for worship on the escarpment at Silver Wattle, 2013.
Photo by Gabbie Paananen.

Introduction

The human species is facing a crisis that will shape the future of humanity on this planet. Climate change is threatening the survival of many living things, and will radically change the way that human societies function. Quakers around the world have rightly been concerned about how to act in the face of this looming catastrophe. What are we called to do?

This lecture argues that in order to act rightly and with courage, Quakers need to strengthen the spiritual bonds of our community.

There are many weighty individuals in our Society who demonstrate extraordinary levels of spiritual courage and commitment. They encourage us to see our Society as a successful force for change in the world, but behind these successes is a Society of Friends that is spiritually 'unwell', because it is disconnected from the vitality of the young. If we look at our Society in Australia, we see that, with the exception of the annual Yearly Meeting gathering, there are almost no children regularly attending Meetings for Worship.

How has our Society reached this crisis point? Many families say that they feel unwelcome or unsupported at Meetings, and have stopped attending, or even resigned from membership. Younger Friends feel that their gifts and leadership are not recognised, and drift away. Older Friends feel exhausted by the administrative burden they carry on behalf of the Society.

All Friends are missing out on the life-affirming joy of intergenerational worship and play.

Our Quaker tradition is built on the energy and clarity of young people. It was young people who carried the message of the 'purifying' Light to a war-torn 17th century Britain. These young people in their teens and early twenties faced physical dangers including beatings, whippings, drowning, jail, starvation and torture and in some cases, death. They demonstrated incredible courage fueled by their commitment to spiritual Truth and by the support that their loving religious community gave them.

Children are important to our Society and to the world, not just for the future, but for the joy and wonder that they share in the present. Children remind us of the value of love, of fun, of the spirituality of play and of God in our bodies. Including children in our worship is not just about preventing Friends from 'dying out', but about reconnecting all of us with 'life's longing for itself'.[2] Without children we are not a Society.

But our generation and many generations before have bequeathed to our children a most horrible inheritance. Ahead is a time of famine, disease, and economic and social instability. Indeed these changes have already begun. We need to equip our children and young people with the tools to survive, to heal and if possible to rebuild our broken world. It is my belief that Quakers are called to deepen our faith now: to strengthen our bonds as a spiritual community and to act from a place of love and truth so that we are ready to act as the world needs us to act.

1. Changing cultures

The most serious disadvantage suffered by children and young people is their invisibility to adults. When this remains unrectified, we are not only failing the children and depriving ourselves of learning from their light, but also keeping ourselves out of hearing distance from God's message through them.[3]

Helen Bayes, 2003

I am known amongst Australian Friends as a 'Compass' Quaker: Not because I have a good sense of spiritual direction, or because I know my own 'centre point', but because I first heard about Quakers on an ABC television series called *Compass*. The show was called *Seeking the Light Within*[4], and led to a rush of new attenders around the country. On that program Sheila Given, a retired teacher from Friends' School, Hobart, spoke about the Quaker approach to children and education:

> *I have been all my life fascinated by children and education. And I believe and always have that a child is not born in original sin but is an original blessing. Has a core spirituality, magnificent mystery inside them and that you build on that.*[5]

Since that first inspiring glimpse of Australian Quakers on television, I have had an enduring interest in the value of children in our Meetings. This may be partly because my husband and I had young children when we first joined. We have had to face the challenge of including them in our worshipping practice from the beginning. It may also be because we were deeply in love with our children when we became Quakers, as all new parents are. Our children looked to us like they knew God. So our learning about early parenthood and about Quakerism was a joint project.

The day after the *Compass* program aired, I rang the number listed under 'Quakers' in the Ballarat phone book. The voice at the other end told me about the Meeting, and what I should expect. Although I was interested, I told her that I didn't think we would be able to come very often because our children would surely disrupt the silence. 'Oh no', she said. 'Quakers love children. They are always welcome at Meeting.'

The role of children in the Society of Friends

Quakers don't like rules, but there are strong guidelines, often framed as questions, which direct our practice in certain directions. These 'Advices and Queries'[6] urge adults to remember our testimony of equality in regard to children:

> *Rejoice in the presence of children and young people in your Meeting and recognise the gifts they bring. Remember that the Meeting as a whole shares a responsibility for every child in its care. Seek for them, as for yourself a full development of God's gifts and the abundant life Jesus tells us can be ours. How do you share your deepest beliefs with them, while leaving them free to develop as the spirit of God may lead them? Do you invite them to share their insights with you? Are you ready both to learn from them and to accept your responsibilities towards them?* [7]

> *Advices and Queries* 19

Children are acknowledged as spiritually equal to adults through the process of Quaker membership. The *Handbook of Practice and Procedure in Australia* states that, 'The child is the responsibility of the Meeting and an integral part of it'. He or she 'may be listed as a child or youth of the Meeting'.[8] Importantly, at any age, a child may wish to become a Member, and would then go through the same process that adult Members go through.

Over the past 40 years, Australian Friends have actively sought to include children more equally in our business and spiritual practice. In 1984, Australia Yearly Meeting (AYM) convened an open session of Regional Meeting Children's Committees as part of a Business session. The Junior Young Friends (JYFs) at this Meeting asked that their 'ministry be accepted in the light of a gathered Meeting and not be commented on by adults'.[9] The recorded minute indicates the significance of this occasion in the recognition of the status of children:

> *We should be sensitive to the need for parents not to be the sole elders on the children's committee. Queries on children should be read aloud in Regional Meetings possibly at least quarterly to keep the corporate responsibility for the children of the Regional Meeting before us. The children should be encouraged to make their own input to the children's Meeting, especially in the case of JYFs who, it is hoped, will take on the major initiative in running their own affairs.*[10]

In 1987, AYM re-established the Yearly Meeting Children's Committee 'to foster the flow of ideas between Regional Meetings to encourage the more effective involvement of children and young people in Meetings'[11] and to 'encourage the formation of links between individual adults and children in the Society'.[12] The committee was very active over the next ten year period, introducing Penn Friends as a way of strengthening relationships between generations[13]; a guide and leaflet for the planning of the Children's Meeting[14]; guidelines for children's programs at AYM gatherings; and producing a Young Friends page for the *Australian Friend.* In 1994, the committee produced a 'Rainbow of Hope' banner for the Friends World Committee for Consultation Triennial Gathering along with a minute asking all Friends to include children more fully in our Quaker life and practice.[15]

At Yearly Meeting 1998, Young Friends and JYFs explained their expectation of respect and participation, in more detail:

> *We would like older Quakers to know that we often feel what we say in Meeting is treated with disrespect. This disrespect either looks like what we have said is inappropriate and is ignored, or that we are gushed over and we feel patronised. We speak because the Spirit moves us. It seems strange that we should be gushed over for being moved by the Spirit. We don't want to stop you from thanking us for our contributions, but we'd like you to address the content rather than the age of the speaker.*[16]

Quaker children expect to be heard, because we encourage them to speak. It is a mark of their upbringing in a non-hierarchical Society such as ours. For some younger Friends, it is a shock when other religious groups do not treat young people in the same way.

> *During my time away I realised that in being a Quaker there were many things I had taken for granted, like that young people are seen as valid*

contributors, are listened to and that there is a desire for dialogue between younger and older members of the Meetings. I expected the same would be the case elsewhere. I learned the hard way that this was not so! [17]

Anna Wilkinson, 2000

The respect that Quakers have for children is most evident at family camps and gatherings. On these occasions, I have seen elderly Friends bend down, take the hand of my children and speak to them encouragingly about their own interests. These offerings of love have left a legacy of incredible self-confidence in my children because they feel acknowledged and loved by people other than their parents.

Clearly, Quakers believe that children and young people carry the Light of God, just as adults do, and that they are entitled to an equal place in our community. So why are we unable to support families and young children to participate more actively in our Society? Why is there such a generational gap between the older Quakers who uphold the Meeting and the families and children who rarely attend?

I went to my first Yearly Meeting in Brisbane when I was 7 months pregnant with my third child. I had high hopes for this event because my experience and reading about Quakers had encouraged me to believe that this would be a time of spiritual renewal and connection for my children and me. In fact, it ended up as a hugely distressing time, because I saw and experienced the gulf between our hopes for including children and the difficulty that our community has in achieving them.

On one particular evening I wondered how I could continue in this Society where my children and I didn't have a place. That night I had an apocalyptic vision in my dreams of a large city (read Society) crumbling to the ground. In the dream, my children and I were the only people in an almost deserted city. We were frightened and saddened by this cold, empty place. We didn't want to leave, but we didn't know what else to do.

How bad is it?

In 2009, the AYM Children and JYF committee conducted a survey of children's Meetings around Australia to find out how many children were attending Meetings, the things that carers and families did in Meetings, what resources were being used, and the challenges and joys that the Meetings had encountered.

At the time of this survey there were 230 children on the Australian Quaker database who were mostly the children of Quaker parents. However the responses to our survey indicated that very few of these children actually attended Meetings. Many Meetings had no children attending at all. Others had a very small number (between 3-6 children) who usually attended monthly. Carers were struggling to manage the planning of appropriate children's programs, as well as finding appropriate carers, and it seemed that parents were generally the ones to shoulder the responsibility for the care of the Meeting's children during Sunday Worship.

In 2012, in response to the problems highlighted by this survey, the AYM Children and JYF committee organised a four day workshop entitled *Bringing Children and JYFs into the Centre of Quaker Life*, which was represented by nominees from all Regional Meetings. Feedback from participants indicated that little had changed since our 2009 survey, and that there were some Regional Meetings that appeared to have no 'children of the Meeting'.[18] Even the Meetings with regular attendance by children and teenagers found it difficult:

> *(There is) a small group of adults carrying most of the responsibility. There are no named members on the children's committee. Non-parents do not get involved with planning, with a few exceptions. There are unfulfilled commitments, and families have different priorities and levels of commitment. Friends in the Meeting have low levels of confidence when it comes to planning for and working with children and JYFs.[19]*

Friends attending the workshop were clear that there was a 'disconnect' between children and adult Quakers especially in regard to worship. They stated in very strong terms that all Australian Friends needed to address this problem urgently in order for the Society of Friends to continue to exist.

A concern of the Backhouse Lecture series

I am not the first Backhouse Lecturer to reflect on the issue of intergenerational segregation in our Quaker community. Elise Boulding, Helen Bayes, Young Friends and others have spoken about the value of including children and young people in our spiritual community and the dangers of excluding the younger generation. The repetition of this theme in the lectures demonstrates that Friends are deeply concerned, that we are yet to resolve the problem and that we are hopeful for a solution.

Our children, Our partners: Elise Boulding (1996)

Throughout her life, Elise Boulding worked as an activist and an academic with an interest in bringing all nations towards peaceful coexistence. She saw relationships with children and young people as being crucial to the success of this movement, and felt that Quakers had the potential to be a part of this change.

In her lecture, subtitled '*a new vision for social action in the 21st century*', Boulding wrote specifically about environmental and social justice projects that were initiated and sustained by children, demonstrating the skills that young people have when they are empowered to act. She argued that Friends 'have some serious visioning to do' in order to become a community that is capable of addressing the needs of the future.

Boulding promoted the inclusion of Young Friends in every Quaker committee as well as mature JYFs in some circumstances. She noted the success of intergenerational gatherings and asked if these ways of being together could also be carried into other Quaker activities, including Meetings for Worship for Business.

Elise Boulding's lecture was, and still is, highly influential for Australian Friends. In the years following the lecture, a number of new initiatives were undertaken in order to include children more fully in the whole of the Meeting: at Yearly Meeting 1997, Friends participated in an all-age worship session; and the nomination of Young Friends on to business committees and Standing Committee has become common practice.

Respecting the Rights of Children and Young People: Helen Bayes (2003)

Helen Bayes has a background as an advocate for children's rights and worked for 15 years for Defence for Children International (DCI). In her lecture she wrote about the interplay of her work as an activist, her leading to work in this field and a descriptive history of the place of children in the early Quaker movement.

She wrote about the change in the Australian Society of Friends after Elise Boulding's lecture, and expressed her disappointment that so many of these initiatives did not continue. She wrote about the abandonment of all-age worship after an initial success in 1997 because a number of individual Friends expressed their dislike of semi-programmed worship. At the local Meeting level, some attempts were made to invite adult Friends to join the children's worship but the invitation was rarely taken up:

> *The plain fact is that we have not been able to sustain the joint adventure which Elise Boulding advocated and which would lead us into rich new spiritual experiences.*[20]

Bayes wrote about the revolutionary attitude that the early Quakers had to the innate spirituality of every person. They considered the 'inward light' or the 'seed' to be divine potential, not something that grew along with physical maturity or life experience. Consequently, Quakers believed that children were born without original sin, eliminating the need for a baptism to 'wash away their sins', and advancing the status of children in the family and the community. Quakers ministered fervently about the need to nurture the spiritual life of children, urging adults to protect children from temptation so that they could live up to their 'divine potential'.

The equality that children were given in this new community empowered them to follow their own leadings, even when they were at odds with the views of the older generation. Consequently, the next generation of adult Quakers chose stricter methods of parenting including physical punishment in some cases in contradiction to the testimony against violence.

Helen encouraged Friends to re-examine the heritage of the early Quaker movement as a model for reinvigorating our adult relationships with children and deepening the quality of worship for the whole community.

Finding our Voice: Young Friends (2010)

Young Friends wrote about their struggle to find a place in the world and in the Society of Friends at a time when they are expected to be independent and to make their own choices.

They valued the example of the early Friends movement; the harsh, exposing Light that they lived by. They valued Meeting for Worship at their own gatherings, and worked to make it accessible to all by scheduling it at a time when others were awake and available. Few Young Friends attended their local Meeting outside of Young Friends gatherings for many reasons including practical difficulties (travel), different priorities, finding Meeting difficult, and not feeling a part of the local Meeting.

They argued that although Quakers valued stillness, sometimes it seemed that membership was 'measured by joining more committees or attending more Meetings'.[21] Young Friends didn't want to do this. They wanted more opportunities for silence.

Many Young Friends wished that they had received a more formal teaching of Quaker processes and practices when they were younger, and felt as though this has contributed to a sense of disengagement from the broader community of Friends.

The lecture finished with Young Friends expressing a sense of hope about the future:

> *The Quaker way offers us all the remarkable chance to create the world we want to see, right here, right now, and have the full support of a loving community.*[22]

Embarking on a Journey

In 1958, Naomi Stillhere noted the declining membership of British Quakers and was led to act. She bought a boat to live in and travelled the inland waterways of Britain sharing the Quaker message with children and others. She used Matthew's gospel as the theme:

> *He called a little child to him, and placed the child among them. And he said: 'Truly I tell you, unless you change and become like little children, you will never enter the kingdom of heaven'.*[23]

She called her ministry *The Celebration of Childhood*. She saw this message as the way forward for an enlivenment of Quaker life.[24] I love this image of a passionate Quaker woman bringing her floating home to new towns and inviting children to join a lively, curious tradition. Stillhere's message was that children are the heart of our faith, not because they are the future, but because they are the embodiment of our faith tradition, and are rooted in Jesus' message of simplicity and humility. Stillhere's journey is a symbolic ministry for Friends, an acknowledgement that the renewal of our Society is about listening to and talking with children.

I see this lecture as another stop on the journey towards living and loving as a whole community. In Australia, this journey was begun with the Business Meeting at Yearly Meeting 1984, and has been taken up by Elise Boulding, Helen Bayes, Young Friends and other Backhouse lecturers.

This lecture is not only about children, just as every other lecture is not only about adults. Clearly, Australian Friends are interested in improving our relationships with children and young people, but we don't yet know how to do it, and we haven't yet realised the level of change that is needed. It has been said that bringing children into the centre of Quaker life will require a culture change for Australian Friends.[25] Changing culture takes time; it is difficult, and uncomfortable. We should not underestimate the work that it will take. But it will lead us to a deeper and richer spiritual life as a community, and consequently as individuals.

And we can look to our Quaker tradition to find some answers.

2. Children of the Light

The Early Quakers called themselves *Children of the Light* among other names. They saw themselves as God's 'children' and knew that Jesus loved little children best of all.[26] In the 17th century, children were at the bottom of the social stratum, and Quakers understood 'living like little children' to mean living as the weakest and the most vulnerable did. Thus they sought out meekness and humility as Jesus taught them to:

Blessed are the poor in spirit,
*   for theirs is the kingdom of heaven.*
Blessed are those who mourn,
*   for they will be comforted.*
Blessed are the meek,
*   for they will inherit the earth.*
Blessed are those who hunger and thirst for righteousness,
*   for they will be filled.*
Blessed are the merciful,
*   for they will be shown mercy.*
Blessed are the pure in heart,
*   for they will see God.*
Blessed are the peacemakers,
*   for they will be called children of God.*
Blessed are those who are persecuted because of righteousness,
*   for theirs is the kingdom of heaven.*[27]

Children of the 17th Century

Childhood as we know it, did not really exist in 17th century England. The average life expectancy was just under 40 years, largely because of the very high levels of childhood mortality. Approximately 14 per cent of children died before they reached the age of one. The first few weeks of life were the most dangerous, and statistically, life became safer as each month and year passed. Poor sanitation, disease and accidents were the most common causes of death for children.[28]

Children were vulnerable to illness, accident, abuse, poverty and exploitation. Childbirth itself was extremely dangerous and many women had more children than they could physically or economically manage. Young babies were often sent to wet nurses, especially if the mother needed to work. Wet nurses were paid per child, and some women fed up to 10 babies at a time. Many of these babies died from inadequate nutrition and starvation. Baby farming was another common, but unregulated practice, where a woman would be paid to care for a baby during the first few years. Many of these children were neglected, exploited or abused.

Unwanted children were often killed or abandoned, and as a consequence, there were large numbers of children living on the streets. Children who were lucky enough to remain in the family home were expected to contribute to the family income, or provide for themselves as soon as they were able. Children took on adult responsibilities and faced dangers that would be considered neglectful in our contemporary Western society. There was little time for indulgences; children needed to work to keep the family alive.

The status of Quaker children

Quakers believed that God spoke directly to everyone, without the need for an intermediary or a church. The Light of God was within all, regardless of class, gender, race or even age; that included children as well as adults. Original sin did not exist, and therefore baptism was redundant. Quaker children were treated as spiritually autonomous individuals, distinct from their parents, and with their own personal relationship with God.

George Fox urged young people to consider themselves as 'the great work of God'. Religious education was taken very seriously among Friends and parents were urged to carefully nurture the 'seed', and to be good models for their tender 'lambs'. The ministry of children was taken as seriously as that of adult Quakers:

Thus the Light was not understood as something that emerged in adulthood, as a product of education and maturity, but God was present and active in the child from the beginning. True ministry could flow from child to adult, as well as from adult to child. Children were brought to Meetings as a matter of course, and all parents were urged to bring them.

Helen Bayes, 2003

Despite the affection that the early Quakers had for their children, family life was often greatly disrupted by the political and spiritual activities of the parents. Children witnessed a great deal of violence first hand, much of it directed against their parents and sometimes themselves. They were expected to take on responsibilities such as running the family home on their own, while their parents travelled in the ministry or were taken to prison.

Some children were born in prison, or lived with their imprisoned parents and cared for them while they were dying. The well-known story of the children of Reading Meeting is a moving testimony to the bravery of these children and also an illustration of the confidence they felt in their own leadership during this difficult time:

> *It was May 1662 and a law had recently been passed outlawing the meeting of Quakers, but the community continued to meet. One evening the adults were seized and taken to prison, and the children woke to find that they alone were responsible for the running of the meeting. They couldn't get inside the Meeting-House as it had been locked up by the police, so they gathered in a granary that belonged to one of the families. They began meeting as usual, but were soon interrupted by the King's soldiers. Sir William Armorer, Justice of the Peace, and Equerry to the King was shocked at the sight; "Quaker brats, holding a conventicle of their own, as if they were grown men and women! Having stopped the earth and gaoled the fox, must we now deal with the litter?" The soldiers beat the boys with sticks and punched and hit them until 'they were black in the face', and the girls were driven away. Even after this frightening experience, the children continued to meet for worship in Reading every Sunday.[31]*

What is remarkable about these Quaker children is not how much responsibility they carried, but that their wisdom was listened to, without discrimination. Children of any age had the potential to be leaders in the Quaker movement, provided they listened for God, and lived up to the Light.

A young movement

From an early age, George Fox was clearly a different child from his peers. At the age of 11, he knew 'pureness and righteousness', and described himself as a serious child, 'being more religiously inward, still, solid and observing beyond his years'.[32] He was well read, especially in theology, church history and the Bible. In his early teens, he stopped going to church because he didn't agree with the theological teachings. Instead, he spent his time walking, reading and thinking. He also fasted, and spent many hours in stillness and silence, often walking at night, as he sought a direction for himself. He left home at 19 years of age to continue his search, and was convinced in his early twenties, after the revelation that Christ spoke to him directly:

> *As I had forsaken the priests, so I left the separate preachers also, and those esteemed the most experienced people; for I saw there was none among them all that could speak to my condition. And when all my hopes in them and in all men were gone, so that I had nothing outwardly to help me, nor could tell what to do, then, oh, then, I heard a voice which said, "There is one, even Christ Jesus, that can speak to thy condition"; and when I heard it my heart did leap for joy.[33]*

From this young man's revelation, grew a movement of mostly young, charismatic men and women who risked their lives to 'live adventurously' as Quakers. Leutke-Stahlman, in her book; *Seventeenth Century Remarkable Quaker Youth*, lists a surprising number of young men, women and even children who contributed to the growth of Quakerism.[34]

Edward Burrough was convinced at the age of 16 after hearing George Fox speak publicly. He was forced to leave the family home after becoming a Quaker, and went on to become an influential preacher and advocate for Quakers in public life. He successfully convinced King Charles II to issue a temporary writ to stop the persecution of Quakers in New England.[35]

William Penn was 13 years of age when he heard the Quaker Thomas Loe say that God could speak directly to the hearts of men and women. Young William felt a sense of déjà vu: he knew it to be true. Later, when he was 15 and at Oxford, Penn was fined for holding private prayer sessions and refusing to attend services at the Puritan chapel. He joined the Quakers when he was 22, against his father's wishes.[36]

James Parnell was convinced at the age of 15 after meeting George Fox in prison. He was described as a very impressive speaker, but it wasn't his voice or his physical presence that carried weight. His small body would often shake and tremble as he spoke in front of large crowds. People teasingly called him 'the quaking boy' or 'little James'. On one occasion, a man was offended by what he said, and struck him on the face shouting: *take that for Jesus Christ's sake!* James replied: *Friend, I do receive it for Jesus Christ's sake.*[37] At the age of 18, James was imprisoned and suffered terribly from neglect. He died shortly afterwards.

Elizabeth Fletcher was 14 years of age in 1653 when she first met Fox. A year later, she travelled with Elizabeth Leavens to preach in Oxford. It was very dangerous for women to travel on their own, so the two Elizabeths wore their hair loose and dressed as men. When they arrived in Oxford, their public preaching angered the scholars so much that the women were beaten and dragged to the water pump, where water was poured over their heads and necks and into their mouths until they almost drowned:

> *Then they took one of them and bound her Knees together, and set her upon her Head, saying 'They would pump at the other End', after which they tied them Arm to Arm, and dragged them up and down the College, and through a Pool of Water, and then they threw Elizabeth Fletcher, who was a young Woman, over a Gravestone into a Grave, by which she received such a Blow on the Side, as she never recover'd to her Death, which was not very long after.*[38]

Later, the women were arrested and ordered to be 'whipt out of the city'.[39] A year later, Elizabeth Fletcher went again to Oxford, this time stripping off her clothes as a sign against the hypocrisy of religious people there.[40] This was not something she found easy to do.[41] Like many other Friends who went naked as a sign, she felt humiliated and frightened by what she felt she had to do, but she did it anyway.

A brief word about nakedness

A number of early Friends practised public nakedness as a metaphor for the spiritual truth of simplicity and vulnerability against the hypocrisy of state and church power. In *Isaiah* 20, God commands Isaiah to take off his sackcloth and walk barefoot and naked for three years. For Isaiah, as well as the 17th century Quakers, nakedness didn't always mean total nudity; it meant removing your outer garments so that your underclothes were visible. Elizabeth Fletcher, Robert Barclay, Solomon Eccles, William Sympson and others felt led to follow Isaiah's example despite their embarrassment and fear. Public displays of nudity were often interpreted as a great blasphemy, especially if demonstrated by women, and attracted a violent response from audiences.

You may have seen the YouTube music video of Jon Watts in Meeting, suddenly becoming inspired to minister. He takes off his clothes – not all of them – and runs out into the sunshine and through the trees. Others from the meeting follow him and it becomes a Meeting for Worship for Semi-Naked Running![42] This song was inspired by a pamphlet *Clothe Yourself in Righteousness: But First Get Naked* written by Maggie Harrison about nakedness as ministry as practised by the early Quakers.[43]

Maggie and Jon have been inspired by the commitment these early Quakers had to make a stand against social injustice, even at the cost of their own dignity and safety. They ask: if we were called to shed our clothing and stand naked before God and before each other, what would we do?

What do these stories mean today?

The important thing about these stories is not that early Quaker children and young people were extraordinary, although to us they seem so. It is that they were part of a loving, supportive movement that empowered them, acknowledged their gifts, and guided them spiritually and practically. Children and young people learned about their Quaker faith through responsibility. They understood that the Society valued them[44] and they felt as though they belonged.[45]

The passion and theatricality of the early Quakers reminds me of the peace movement in the 1970s, the environment movement today, and the political protests of the 'Arab Spring'. Political and social change is so often driven by the energy and organisational skills of the young, combined with the support and experience of older activists.

What would our community be like if we gave our young people the support that these young people had? Do we have the strength to hold them as they act radically according to their leadings? Do we give children and teenagers the tools to act with love and courage? Most importantly, do we provide a loving community from which their energy can spring forth into the world?

3. Getting our priorities wrong

Contemporary Quakers in the Western world face different challenges from our forebears in the 17th century. In so many ways, we are sheltered from real hardship; from the reality of death, from the dull ache of an empty belly, from the deprivations of war and the humiliation of poverty. Many of us believe that we can control our lives and our environment. We so often forget our privilege and the damage our unthinking consumption does to the planet we share with seven billion other people. Not only is this way of thinking and living irresponsible, I think it does us more harm than we realise, particularly when it comes to living as a community.

In many traditional societies, family and tribal structures are centred around the care of children. Children are seen as integral to the whole community because they represent the joy of new life and because they carry forth the cultural identity of the group. However, in our privileged, Western culture we separate ourselves from children and their chaotic, messy needs. Most people have no real exposure to children until they have their own, and have to learn the essential skills of child rearing in isolation. Caring for young children can be a profoundly lonely experience.

I remember soon after my first child was born, I was totally unprepared for the hours of feeding, washing, waiting, and cleaning and the incredible tiredness that

I felt. I had no idea how to deal with this wilful little person I had given birth to. The advice I read in books seemed to be written about babies quite different from mine. I was resentful of the fun that everyone else seemed to be having outside my window, and I grieved for the life I thought I had lost forever. I knew that some of my friends saw motherhood as a step backwards; that I was somehow less serious about my career, about my feminist ideals. Not only that, everything was so difficult with a child. Even getting into the city with a pram seemed impossible. It was easier to stay at home, away from other people and just get through the day.

Why do we expect new parents to go through one of the most difficult times of their life with so little practical and emotional support? Why do 'stay at home' mothers so often experience this demotion in their social status when they are doing the important work of bringing up children to be ready for our difficult future? If we value our human society, then surely it should be a priority to support those who work so hard to bring up our newest people? Why do we have our priorities so skewed?

Do what I say, not what I do

We Quakers do not exist in a bubble; like all people we are influenced by the attitudes and expectations of the society we are a part of. What is the character of this largely secular society and how does it regard children? What are the underlying values that shape our children beyond family life? In what ways are we complicit in upholding these values even when we disagree with them?

When our children are young, we try to teach them key values that will set them up for an ethical life. We teach them the importance of treating others with respect, the value of sharing, that people are more important than things, and that you should stand up for what you believe in. However, as they get older, they are likely to see that very few adults actually live out these values.

Instead, they may come to learn that:
- Being successful is important, especially in a financial sense
- Being attractive is essential (or no one will like you)
- Greed is okay, or maybe even good
- Excitement is important, even when it is violent
- Getting is more important than giving
- Instant gratification is our right.[46]

These values (if you can call them that!) are largely driven by the advertising industry, which has become an integral part of the economic system that supports our wealthy lifestyles. Marketing is so much a part of our everyday lives that many people think we are immune to its influence. I don't think so. I think the saturation of advertising – on the television, in the newspaper, on the roads, on the streets, in shopping centres and on the T-shirts we wear – encourages us to see that these messages are normal: Yes, I could be better looking if I just … yes I could have an easier life if I just … yes I do deserve that indulgence because … The all-pervasive advertising industry joins 'together in a loud and seductive chorus of entitlement and invites us to sing along'.[47]

We are not always strong enough to resist the consumerism that is at the forefront of so many of our social interactions, and neither are our children. In fact, advertising is increasingly being aimed at children because companies understand that if they build brand loyalty with the young, then they will have them for life.[48] Marketers target the particular vulnerabilities of each age group, and the 'tweenies' (aged eight to twelve) are often the most susceptible to aspirations of 'cool', 'sexy', and famous. Advertising culture seeks to differentiate children's desires from those of their parents, and may pit one generation against another in order to gain more purchasing power.[49]

Hugh Mackay argues that our desire for control and perfection has had a particularly negative effect on children who are brought up to 'believe in themselves' as part of the self-esteem movement. These children are crippled by their unrealistic expectations of life and struggle to deal with the responsibilities of adulthood.[50]

Australian parents say they would like to spend more time with their children and spouses and that they are troubled by the overly materialistic life that their children lead. They also say that they would like their children to be exposed to less advertising.[51] So why aren't parents taking control of these cultural forces? Are they just too powerful, or too tempting?

A toxic childhood?

Despite a growth in economic prosperity in Western countries, and the widespread availability of high quality health care, education and social services, our children are doing less well on 'key indicators such as health, development and well-being'[52] than in the past. In fact, on some measurements, the overall health of children and youth is worsening and the gap between the poorest and richest children is widening. Children are less likely to die young, but illnesses such as asthma, diabetes, obesity, intellectual disabilities and psychological problems are all rising. As are behavior problems such as attention deficit disorder and hyperactivity, levels of substance abuse, and rates of teenage pregnancies. Rates of assault and rape by young people have increased and perpetrators appear to getting younger than ever before.[53]

Dr Fiona Stanley, an epidemiologist noted for her advocacy on behalf of children, and Australian of the Year in 2003, suggests that a number of changes over the past 30-40 years have been at least partly responsible for these poor outcomes in relation to the health of our children. Declining birth rates, globalisation and its effect on economic systems at all levels, increased women in the workforce, changes in family structure, increased consumption and technologies have all played a part in disrupting the traditional networks that once supported the development of children in our society.[54]

Changing technologies have had a profound impact on the leisure habits of children and teenagers. Australian children from the ages of 5-14 spend more time watching television than any other leisure activity.[55] The jury is out on whether violent television shows have a detrimental effect on children or cause children to become violent; these children are usually influenced by a range of factors including their home environment, access to other modes of play, social skills and possible learning or behavioural issues.[56] However there is less doubt about the negative consequences of excessive screen time on a child's developmental health. Children who watch a lot of television and digital games spend less time on physical activity: they do less homework and work around the house and do not do as well academically. There is also evidence to suggest that because they spend less time in 'free' play, they are less creative and less skilled at problem solving. Richard Louv, in his book *Last Child in the Woods,* suggests that children who are disconnected from nature are disadvantaged on a number of levels including a 'diminished use of the senses, attention difficulties, and high rates of physical and emotional illnesses'.[57]

Many parents contain their children in 'safe' indoor environments because they want to protect their children from the dangerous world that they see so vividly described in the media. However, there is no evidence to suggest that violent crimes towards children have increased, although increased anxiety by parents about the risks of 'stranger danger' has led to a marked decrease in the levels of physical activity by children.[58]

Louv argues that time in natural settings is not only good for children's bodies and minds, but that it is also a spiritual necessity.[59] Children love playing outside, they love playing in trees, getting wet, kicking piles of leaves, building shelters, chasing birds, and watching clouds roll by; and this unstructured play is good for them. It is an essential part of their spiritual practice.

As a child, I liked to sit high up in a gum tree in my back yard. My father built me a rope ladder and I would climb as high as I could – sometimes with a book – and then I would sit above my house and my neighbourhood and look at the world around me. Sometimes I would sit there for hours. I liked being close to the sky, in a place without walls, where my perspective was changed by the view in front of me. It was my space.

Nurturing leadership

If we want to see our children develop the capacity to shape the world they are part of, we must encourage their physical, emotional and spiritual autonomy. It might mean that they make some mistakes, or that our usual way of doing things is disrupted for a time. But the biggest challenge for adults, especially parents, is whether we can let go of control over our children. Adults tend to feel quite uncomfortable with children who ask questions, or do things 'differently'. We may be polite and respectful to adults who are odd or eccentric, but rarely do we give this kind of leeway to children. I have seen parents draw pictures for their children to 'help' them do it better. I have seen mothers laugh at their boys if they choose to wear pink or flower patterns in public. I have seen parents tell their girls to stop shouting, getting dirty, or engaging in rough play because it was not 'lady-like'.

Schools are especially intolerant of difference when it interrupts the routines of the institution. For creative children, this can be soul-destroying:

> *The prison-like aspects of my school were taken for granted. Of course we were ranked, compared to our peers, and given certain privileges according to our ranking. Of course the timing of events throughout the day wasn't based on or considerate of our needs and comfort levels. Of course we couldn't go to the*

bathroom without permission. Of course we were obligated to pledge allegiance to the flag each morning. Of course we were threatened and intimidated into behaving in a macro-manageable way. Of course! How else would the institution function! If we had more freedom we would only abuse it. I saw other students laughed at and shamed by students and teachers alike for questioning the fairness of school policies and the 'right' of students to be considered in the decision making process.[60]

Jon Watts, 2007

The secular culture we live in encourages young people to value the trivial rather than striving for integrity. For young people who choose to live differently, to go against the tide, it can feel very lonely. These brave young people need a community that supports them to stand up against the emptiness of the status quo. Our Quaker community offers a supportive space through the discipline of silent worship, of group discernment, of living our actions; these are the things that nurture integrity. But discipline takes practice. If we are to offer these gifts to our children and young people, they need to experience them regularly. Not just from time to time or as the final 15 minutes of Meeting for Worship, but as a practice they can own for themselves that gives them a sense of belonging to the larger body of Friends, and that speaks to their condition as young Quakers in a changing world. As things stand, our community is denying our children and young people the opportunity to grow up as Quakers. We are shutting them out of our traditions at a time when they need them most.

How important is Quakerism to us?

For traditional indigenous communities, the passing on of spiritual culture was essential to the survival of the group. Spiritual practice included maintaining and sharing knowledge about the changing environment, about the best place for water, about how to find good hunting, about the best plants for eating, and so on. Spirit and life were intertwined and tradition was the structure through which the old and the young shared the ongoing responsibility of keeping their community alive.

Do we see the ongoing practice of our spiritual faith as an essential part of our survival into the future? Or is our spirituality more like a lifestyle choice? These are important questions because the value we place on our faith will drive the commitment we bring to including children in our spiritual practice. If we think faith is essential, for us and for the world, then it must also be a priority for us to include our children in our traditions and practices so that they can carry this faith forward into the future.

I am not an evangelist; I don't think everyone should be a Quaker. I don't even think that everyone should be religious. The planet does not need us to believe in God. Spirit will continue to work through the Earth and through us whether we are believers or not. But experiencing the Spirit wakes us up to a more authentic life, and brings us closer to nature and to each other. It inspires us to love; it urges us to be brave and selfless, gentle and courageous. Without these qualities, we will not survive the next difficult phase of human history.

Easter Peace Eggs from Silver Wattle Quaker Centre Easter Family Gathering, 2013. Photo by Gabbie Paananan.

4. Reflections of Light

O how beautiful is the spring in a barren field, where barrenness and deadness fly away. As the spring comes on, the winter casts her coat and the summer is nigh. O, wait to see and read these things within. You that have been as barren and dead and dry without sap; unto you the Sun of Righteousness is risen with healing in his wings and begins to shine in your coasts.[61]

James Parnell at 18 or 19 years of age,
Epistle to Friends from prison

Early Quakers saw that the Light was present in all people from the moment of birth, until the end of life. They understood that the Spirit did not change with experience, but they did not ignore the spiritual nurture of the young. Parents were encouraged to tenderly guide young children into a life of faith and Light at the same time as respecting their individual relationship to God.

Contemporary Quakers seem to be caught in a balance of indecision about how to support the spiritual development of our young people: Should we trust children and young people to find their own path or should we teach them about God according to our traditions so that they know where to begin?

Ideally, we would do both. But how?

Finding the Light within

Before we can support the spiritual independence of young people, we need to acknowledge that they are spiritual beings in their own right. I think this is not well appreciated by most adults. Even Quakers, who value the Spirit in all people, can sometimes be patronising or dismissive of children's spiritual experiences.

I am convinced that all children are innately spiritual from the moment they are born. They have their own experience of the Spirit, including their own modes of worship, of expression, of joyful celebration. Young children don't seem to separate these experiences from their day-to-day lives. They seem to accept that wonder is all around them, that love is a miracle, and that the beginning of the day is a moment of celebration.

Children also have 'black' times, when joy and Light seem a long way away. Most are able to seek comfort in the arms of people who love them, but some have to face great hardship and even horror on their own. These children must find great strength and resilience in order to survive these experiences, and remarkably, most of them do.

In short, children experience God in a range of ways under many different circumstances, just as adults do. It is just as difficult to define children's spirituality as it is to define adult spirituality. I cannot accurately describe a child's view of God in this lecture because each child, and each adult is a unique manifestion of God's grace and is beyond categorisation.

Instead, I would like to describe worshipping experiences that I have shared with children in which I have seen God speak powerfully through young bodies.

Belonging to the Meeting

The silent Quaker Meeting for Worship can be challenging for children (and many adults), but there are many children who enjoy this time of stillness. In fact, some of my most profound experiences have been in Meetings shared with children. At the Easter family camp at Silver Wattle Quaker Centre in 2013, we had an early morning Meeting on the escarpment that overlooks the homestead and the magnificent lake and the distant wind farms. The glory of God was as clear as the view. This Meeting went for a full hour with children from 4–15 years of age as well as adults.

Another memorable Meeting I shared at Silver Wattle was one that was led by the children. We had planned the structure of the Meeting the day before, including where we could sit, how we would make everyone feel included and comfortable, various activities and their symbolic meanings, and logistical stuff. The children were very keen to meet around the old pine tree near the front entrance of the property. The children loved to play in this tree – it had room for all of them; the older ones liked to climb high up into the branches, and the younger children played among the roots. It's a tree that built community between the children.

Asher Lloyd at Yearly Meeting, Adelaide (2010). Photographer unknown.

The journey of this Meeting was to walk as a group out onto the lake and choose a special object that reminded us of God within. We walked in silence, except for some singing, led by the children and one or two adults. After some time on the lake looking closely at rocks and grasses on the lake bed, we all walked back to the 'kids tree', where there were chairs and a rug already set up. Crayons and paper were laid out so that people were able to minister through drawing as well as through silence or vocal ministry. Some people wrote poems.

After the hour had passed, I tried to finish the Meeting, as we had planned, but it was not over. So we returned to silence and the children and adults continued worshipping for another 20 minutes. The children had been responsible for the preparation and the leading of this Meeting. They chose the site, and the journey of the worship. They

An all-age Meeting on the escarpment behind the Silver Wattle Quaker Centre, at the Easter Family Gathering 2013. Photo by Gabbie Paananen.

29

were actively involved, and understood the symbolic meaning of each element. They respected the rule of silence and saw it as their own. That was why time had no meaning at this Meeting.

Children in the 'kids tree' at Easter Family Gathering 2013, Silver Wattle Quaker Centre. Photo by Andrew Bray.

Faith and Experience

There is a body of theological research that suggests that children move through stages of understanding God and religion in their lives. The 'faith stages' theory loosely aligns with Piaget's stages of cognitive development, Erikson's psychosocial stages of growth and Kohlberg stages of moral development. The author of the theory, James Fowler, nominates general age ranges for each stage, although the progression can vary from person to person.

Stage 0: Primal or Undifferentiated (0-2 years)
builds a sense of trust or distrust in the Divine / universe depending on the security of her environment.

Stage 1: Intuitive-Projective (3-7 years)
engages with religion through stories, images, experiences and people she engages with.

Stage 2: Mythic-Literal (primary school age years)
understands religion through symbols, which may be taken literally, and will experience the universe as just and reciprocal.

Stage 3: Synthetic-Conventional (adolescence)
develops personal identity and conforms to religious authority

Stage 4: Individuative-Reflective (mid-twenties to late thirties)
open to faith complexities, but may include personal struggle

Stage 5: Conjunctive (mid-life crisis)
integrates apparent paradoxes and complexities of faith

Stage 6: Universalising
loving, compassionate attitude to humanity

At first glance, this structural approach to religious development challenges the Quaker view that children are born knowing God. However, I think we can make a distinction between spirituality (the Light), which does not change through time; and faith, which is a cognitive understanding of the Spirit and how we live up to it. Clearly, children and adults continue to learn about their relationship with God as they grow older. However, the Spirit itself does not mature. No matter how you understand and describe God, the mystery of the Spirit remains unchanged and unchanging.

Nevertheless, I find this linear model reductive. I have witnessed young children in what Fowler describes as stage 6 'universalising', move quickly into Stage 4 'individuative-reflective' and then onto stage 2 'mythic literal'. The all-age Meeting for Worship that I have just described is a good example of the fluidity of children's spiritual understanding. We all have different ways of coming to terms with God, and we should respect this very personal process as much in children as we do in adults.

That of God within
The secular culture we live in can influence children away from speaking about their spiritual life with others by the time they are 10 years of age.[63] However it seems that children of many faith backgrounds, including those from atheist families, appear to value prayer and see it as something that helps them understand and deal with life, especially during difficult times.[64]

Spiritual practice holds great meaning for children, and they seek it out in their own ways, even when they don't necessarily speak about it. Some children may say that they don't believe in God, but still value the peace and space of spiritual practice. Our faith is one of experience rather than words; 'the letter kills, but the Spirit gives life'.[65] We should encourage children to trust this indescribable experience, rather than trying to fit it into the adult concepts of spirituality that we are comfortable with.

If we are to value our children's spiritual lives, then we must be prepared to see them as individuals with their own idiosyncratic way of living in the Spirit. We can only do this when we get to know them well – by spending one-on-one time with them. We may need to move out of the adult worship and into the children's space from time to time. We may need to broaden our understanding of what prayer is. We may have to give up our usual ways of doing things in order to be part of a whole-of-Meeting journey towards integrated, openly shared worship.

Emily, Rose and Miles Bray painting the rain on a rainy day in Ballarat after many years of drought. Photo by Tracy Bourne.

Miles Bray enjoying the fully grown spring onion that he planted as a seed. Photo by Tracy Bourne.

5. Our tangible link with eternity

Children are our tangible link today with eternity. They are God's restoration of the human creation, the very reincarnation of what God wants for human life on Earth.

Helen Bayes, 1994

When my children were born, I was overwhelmed by the passion of their love for me. They loved me deeply from the moment they drew air. They searched for me. They strained to learn the features of my face. As they grew older, their love was different; the need was not as strong, but still they loved me unconditionally. It is a gift they continue to give. My children teach me how to love and how to willingly put my own needs aside for love. Parenting has brought immeasurable joy, compassion and discipline into my life.

In 2005, I lost a child when I was 24 weeks pregnant. We don't know why I went into premature labour. I had already given birth to two full-term babies who were healthy by all measures. This early labour came very quickly without prior warning and left my husband and me in deep shock. It took me a very long time to recover from this event. My grief was profound – it shook me to my foundations. I lost confidence, withdrew into myself, and felt as raw and skinless as a peeled grape.

It was hard to pinpoint what it was I was grieving. I hadn't seen him or held him while he was alive, but I had held him in my body. We named him Tony because he was quite the dancer in utero and we had been watching the musical *West Side Story* at the time. I felt that he and I were spiritually connected in a way that I have no language for. When I lost him, and began the long process of recovery, I felt that my grief was biological, physical. I had no control over it.

Before he died, I had been a very active person. I enjoyed the busyness of work and public life and I found the early years of breastfeeding, sleeplessness, caring for and entertaining toddlers very difficult. I told myself this was because I wasn't a 'maternal' sort of person. I was more like the blokes. But then I lost a baby, and I lost a part of myself. Losing Tony made me realise that I was maternal because I was a mother. It had nothing to do with how 'good' I thought I was. He taught me that my mother-love is boundless. Loving my children was an impulse that I couldn't control. I loved all of my children from the moment I knew I was carrying them.

Since I lost Tony, I've come to see that all children ask us to move away from judging ourselves as 'not good enough' to care for them. They don't judge us at all. They just want us to be with them, to see them for who they are and to care for them. Children remind us that we are loving, and lovable people. They show us that being lovable is not about being important or powerful or beautiful. It is about being there; it is about opening yourself up to the present. A young baby demands that you care for her and she has many strategies to ensure that this happens – crying, smiling, gurgling, learning, touching. Few of us can look into the face of an engaged and happy child and not be changed. This gift of love – pure, open and trusting – is a gift that is freely given back and forth, from child to adult.

Children teach us
To be curious
To wonder
To play
They teach us to delight in the world
They teach us about simplicity
They teach us that our lives are not all about us!

Our relationships with children are not always easy. Parents can find the endless slog of early childhood especially wearing – with the lack of sleep and the constant demands for attention and discipline that young children make. Older children challenge parents in different ways as they assert their independence from the family.

My three children are very different from each other, and quite different from me. We are always working on building respectful attitudes to each other, especially when we are in conflict. As a parent, I've learned a lot about patience and persistence. I've learned that sometimes I need to put my foot down, and sometimes I should just shut my mouth.

I've learned, and am still learning about the value of apologising and forgiving. I have learned that I need to include my children in the experiment of maintaining a balance between their safety and their right to an independent life. I don't always get it right, and sometimes I am out of my depth; but my children are resilient and usually get over any mistakes I make.

Loving ourselves

Young children love themselves: completely and unashamedly. They love their own bodies, they love to move, to dance, to learn through touch. If a child loves you, she will want to hold you and touch you, and she will trust that you like her body because that is who she is.

I have a wonderful memory of each of my very little children emerging from their bath, clean, dry and warm, and then running up and down the hallway stark naked. They would laugh and scream with joy as they ran; they loved to be liberated from the restriction of nappies and clothing.

We lose that physical self-love as we get older. We are taught to distrust our bodies, and we become scared to touch other people. I don't always hug people that I love – sometimes I'm not sure what they will think of me. Am I invading their space? Maybe they don't like me back?

If the early Quakers saw nakedness as a way to shed the cultural signifiers that we use to prop up our fragile egos, then surely children are the leaders of this movement today! Not only do they love being naked, they are more prepared to take risks and live adventurously than we are. They are more flexible and more curious. They show us that the truth does not come through bitter experience, cynicism or a superior attitude to life. They show us that we get closest to the truth when we strip these things away, when we make ourselves vulnerable, when we recognise our weaknesses and forgive ourselves for that; when we become spiritually naked.

When Jesus asked us to become more like the little children, is this what he meant? If so, we need to open ourselves up to a shared truth-telling; to let children see us as we really are, and to do the same for them.

Nurturing social activists

Young people are at the centre of any political movement because they have the energy, curiosity, social connections and physical strength to challenge the status quo. They don't have the burden of lived history reminding them that change is hard, or 'just can't be done'. They want to be part of making the world a better place. But politically active young people don't just come from nowhere. They come from families or environments that nurture social and political awareness and action. This should not just be up to parents; this is the job of all adults, and children, Junior Young Friends (JYFs) and Young Friends (YFs). We all need to create a space that feeds the curiosity and compassion of young people so that when they are emotionally, physically and spiritually ready, they can act.

Young people teach us that change is important, and ongoing, and that we are all a part of it. They teach us that we don't have to do all the work – that others will continue to fight for justice on our behalf when we are not able to. They teach us that the Spirit is a force that flows through all living things, and that we do not know where it will take us:

> *Young Friends can be a transforming power in today's history. Much has changed since the 17th Century, but Truth remains constant throughout all ages. Our time is now. Our revolution starts today. Let us each fully and honestly submit to the Light within and encourage others to do likewise, getting to know one another in that which is eternal. "Whoever sows to the Spirit, shall reap of the Spirit. So let us not get tired in doing good, because if we do not give up, we shall eventually reap!"*

Francisco Gonzales, 2008

6. A celebration of childhood

Participation and partnership involves working in such a way that the traditional power balance between generations shifts in favour of young people taking up more responsibility, and in consequence developing personally, socially and spiritually. It is not an abdication of responsibility, rather it is a change from a relationship of dependence to one of partnership. It is a way of relating that demands our full acceptance of their autonomy, independence and individuality.

Sandy Parker, 2000

What is the reason for the absence of children in our Meetings? Some Friends say it is because of the difficulty of silent worship. Others suggest that the contemporary, digital, screen based culture that we live in has drawn children away from the simplicity of Quaker practice. Others argue that the busyness of family life makes it difficult for them to attend regular Meetings.

Whatever the reason, it doesn't have to be like this. As a community we can welcome families and young people. We need them. And families need us. Children need to learn the disciplines of worship and listening inwardly. We must prepare our children for witness and service in their lives. If we create a spiritual, communal worshipping space in which children are welcomed, then their families will come too. But in order to do this, our Society of Friends will need to change.

I don't know what this change will be like, but I am sure it will be more fun, more spontaneous, more diverse and more enriching for all Friends if children are at the centre.

Britain Yearly Meeting has produced a challenging policy document called A Theological Basis for Children and Young People's Participation in Quaker Decision-Making which outlines the Quaker tradition as one that justifies the inclusion of children:

- We are a priesthood of all believers that necessarily includes children and young people.
- Quakers believe in the equality of all human beings, which means that all people of all ages are entitled to be a part of worship, play and business.
- We need to educate through nurture so that children and young people are able to understand the unique ways in which we discern the will of God.
- Children's religious experience is important and valuable to our community of Friends. We need to encourage them to develop skills and confidence in Quaker practice by providing opportunities to engage with Quaker Meetings and business.
- By including children in our Meetings, we acknowledge that living in community is 'an exercise in selflessness', and that we may be required to do things in unfamiliar ways. This can be difficult for younger and older Friends, but is ultimately strengthening to the group.

My family attends a very small Meeting – we usually only have between 4-10 people attending on two Sundays of the month. Often, our family forms the majority of the Meeting. There have been times when we have struggled to bring our children to Meeting, and where we have not felt supported as a family. However, it is important to say that whenever we have raised these concerns with our Meeting we have always been heard, and the whole Meeting has been engaged with the dilemma of how to include all of us in meaningful worship.

The discussions haven't always been easy. Like all Meetings, we have had to balance a desire amongst Friends for quiet contemplative silence, and an acknowledgement of the value of an inclusive and robust worship where the children feel welcome. Our current solution is to have a children's Meeting on fourth Sundays, with a Quaker leading the program and a paid carer as the second person. On second Sundays, we include the children in the whole Meeting for the full hour, and they read or play quietly or make craft. All of the children endeavour to spend some time in stillness and silence. My 14-year-old daughter aims to spend 20-30 minutes, while my 11 and 7 year old will aim for 10-15 minutes.

One Meeting

For some Meetings, it is better to include the children in Meeting for Worship for the full hour. For others, it is more suitable to provide a children's Meeting for Worship away from the adult Meeting. These two options can be seen as the end points of a continuum in which Meetings include children in the spiritual life of the Meeting whether they are present in the same room as the adults or in an alternative space.

In many Meetings, there can be a subtle, underlying sense that the adult Meeting is the 'main' Meeting and the children's Meeting is its satellite. What if the children's Meeting were considered the heart and centre of the whole Meeting? What would that look like? How could your Meeting demonstrate this? Perhaps the adults and children can swap rooms sometimes? Or perhaps the adults can begin with the children, and then leave for adult worship in another room.

These choices all say something about the roles that we play in the larger community – and we need to consider carefully what our actions are saying – because they speak more deeply than our words. Remember that the Meeting is ONE Meeting even if it is being held in different rooms.

The Children's Meeting for Worship

A separate Children's Meeting for Worship works well when there are a number of qualified carers available to organise and run the program. Children often prefer to worship with their peers, and a good program can attract more families to join the Meeting. Children's carers need to be supported by the whole Meeting: by providing appropriate resources, by assisting with the preparation of the program, and by offering training if needed.

In Australia, we have a number of smaller, isolated Meetings that find it difficult to support a regular children's Meeting. But size needn't be a barrier to families participating in worship. In fact, the flexibility of a smaller Meeting may make it easier to adjust the Meeting for Worship to suit the needs of everyone.

Regardless of size, the whole Meeting should ensure that there is regular communication between the children and adults and that the communication is not just adults to children. Children need an opportunity to express their interests and concerns in ways that suit them. Adults can benefit from encouraging children to share their spiritual experiences with the whole of the worshipping community.

One common routine is for children to join the adult Meeting at some point to report on what they did during their own Meeting. Delightful as this time is, it is worth remembering that many children are easily overwhelmed in adult spaces, and they can feel as though they don't have permission or the knowledge to speak with authority about God. Meetings will benefit from fostering other modes of worship-sharing in order to listen and learn from children.

Children's Meeting should also include significant amounts of silent worship, depending on the age and experience of the children. Younger children are capable of about 10 minutes of silence, and older children and teenagers can usually manage 15-30 minutes. However, I have seen ten-year-old children sit quietly and comfortably for a full hour. Silent worship requires practice. It can be difficult for all Friends, including adults, and it is hardest for those who lack experience. Eventually, older children and teenagers will want to stay in the adult Meeting for longer and longer periods of time. This is easier if they feel welcome and encouraged by adult Friends.

In the past few years, some Friends have been unclear or anxious about legislative changes in regard to the care of children. At the same time, the abuse of children in religious institutions has become a prominent issue in the media, and in our own Society too. We all want to prevent predatory behaviour towards children. Consequently, there are Quaker processes and state legislation that we must all comply with if we are to spend time with the children during Meetings and gatherings.

However, I am concerned these requirements may be preventing some Friends from assisting with the children. I suspect that some men in particular may feel a loss of confidence in the value they bring to children's play and worship. There is a danger that our children may think that we don't want to be with them, because of rules that we can't explain. Despite these concerns, we need to accept that these regulations are not going to go away. We must come to terms with the extra administrative work required, and make it a priority. With a small amount of research, most Friends will find that the requirements are not as onerous as they first thought.

All-age worship

In Chapter 4, I wrote about some of the joyful all-age worship that I have shared with children. Most adult Friends who engage with these experiences willingly find they are as spiritually enriching as the children do. Nevertheless, some Quakers seem to be resistant to multigenerational worship. They find the children distracting, or wish that they were 'better behaved' during the silence. Some Friends are concerned that all-age worship goes against our silent tradition. However, all-age worship is rarely a fully programmed Meeting. Generally it will include a prompting for all Friends to respond to, and a range of ways in which Friends can reflect, including silence, drawing, singing, craft and worship sharing.

The content of the all-age Meeting, and the modes of worship sharing should be determined beforehand by Friends nominated by the Meeting. The prompting should be open enough to allow Friends of many backgrounds to find something useful for them. Stories (Biblical, Universalist, Humanist), pictures, images, and songs often have layered meanings and can provide opportunities for group reflection on the mysteries of spiritual and Christian traditions.

Quakers do not believe that God belongs in a church, or only in a specific practice. God is in all of us, at all times. We are also open to many ways of worshipping, although we may have a preference for a particular place, time and manner of worship. At the same time, I think it is important for all of us to 'shake up' our usual ways of being in the Spirit from time to time. Habit is not always beneficial for the seeker. Comfort can shield us from the 'adventurous' path.

Developing the discipline to sit with God in a more active Meeting should not be too difficult for the experienced Quaker, and can very useful in our lives beyond the Meeting. Children may wiggle a little, and are likely to make some noise, but that needn't distract the Meeting. We are not as disturbed by cars driving past, or the tree branch knocking on the window; perhaps the quiet noises of settled children might become part of the natural soundscape of the Meeting?

Learning about Quaker traditions

When thy children ask thee any questions of this nature – What is God, where he dwells; or whether he sees them in the dark – do not reject it; but wait to feel somewhat of God raised in thee, whether the question be put forth in sensibility or in vanity; and which can give thee an advantage of stirring the good... As for praying, they will not need to be taught that outwardly; but if a true sense be kindled in them, though ever so young, from that sense will arise breathings to him that begat it, suitable to their state; which will cause growth and that sense of life in them.

Isaac Penington, 1665

Children do need to learn about Quaker traditions, and as a community we have not always done this well. Part of the problem seems to be that we do not have a clear approach to the education of Quaker children. We appear to be confused about how much we should allow children to find their own faith, and how much we should lead them. Is this part of our 21st century scepticism, or are we actually unsure of our own beliefs? Are we scared of offending others who may disagree with our theology?

When I say education, let me be clear that I am not talking about teaching children to love God – they already have that deep within them. What I mean is that they need to learn how their elders, and our Quaker ancestors worshipped, and what they did to fight injustice and promote peace. Hearing stories from the past reveals the ways in which we can manage the present and imagine the future. Children need to hear these stories so that they can understand the living presence of the Spirit in our contemporary world.

Clearly, one of the sticking points is that we are divided as a community about our own theology; Christian, Universalist, Humanist? This is not helping our children, and the anxiety that is behind this concern suggests that we don't trust our children to determine their own faith journey.

We must remember that children are 'Children of the Meeting'. On Sundays, or during gatherings they are the responsibility of us all, not just their own parents. Parents must trust that the Meeting will make the right decision about spiritual direction for the children's Meeting for Worship.

If we truly respect children as spiritually autonomous, we can offer them a diversity of spiritual influences and know that they will make the right choice. I hope that Meetings are able to educate children about the Bible, and about other spiritual and religious cultures in a way that the children can respectfully question what is written. Spiritual questioning is at the heart of our faith – we have advices and queries, not rules – and we should encourage this attitude with our children too.

There is so much wisdom within the Bible, but there is also contradiction, and writings that are so old it can be hard for us to understand what they mean today. However, we are a Christian tradition, whether you personally identify as a Christian or not, and our children need to develop their own relationship to this book and to the story of Jesus. His example was very important to the early Friends, and led them to create a movement that was both political and religious. In my mind, the contemporary Society of Friends is not so different: We are a radical, Spirit led, grass roots movement. All of these things belong together and you can't separate Jesus and his example from the story of Quakers.

This attitude of spiritual discipline and political action is what we, and our children, need to encourage within each other as we face a future of deepening injustice and loss. Our community, including our children, needs to understand how to connect to the strength of the Spirit so we are all emboldened to act as we need to act. It's not just about committees and minutes; they are only one part of our worshipping life. Worshipping deeply and creatively as a community will enliven our committees and give us the energy to manage what we need to do.

Giving responsibility to children

Elise Boulding, in her Backhouse Lecture, argued that we should include children more in business and decision-making processes. Sometimes this doesn't work because we have not chosen the right task for our young people. Nominating Friends of any age should include an acknowledgement of their particular gifts and an understanding of their readiness for the task, taking into account how busy they are, and what other support they may need. When you consider nominating a child to take on a task in the Meeting, look to the person, to their gifts, and let that guide your choice of tasks. Nominating younger Friends is also a declaration of our confidence in their readiness to take on more responsibility in the Meeting:

> *Over the years that we went to Meeting, I never had more than two or three other kids who were the same age as me, but the adults of the Meeting who were not my parents took a strong interest in talking with me about spiritual*

and theological topics during First-day school time. As I became a teenager, the Meeting started to recognise my gifts and expertise in certain areas. I became a member when I was 12, and was then invited to join the Worship and Ministry Committee when I was 14. My longtime First-day school teacher picked me up and took me home again for all of this committee's Meetings, since he was on it too. At this point, I had an identity as a member of our Meeting's community who had responsibilities, and it was a completely separate identity from that of my parents, who happened to be extremely committed and involved members in their own right. If one has no ownership of what is happening in a community, one is generally not very interested or invested in the process of making the community function. This is just as true for people under 14 as it is for those over 14. But one cannot simply issue a general invitation to join a committee and expect numerous 7 or 12 year olds to respond eagerly. It is up to experienced Friends to make the effort to get to know each of the young folk individually, and to then consider and evaluate what gifts, skills, expertise, or presence that person has that they could contribute to the Meeting - and then to figure out the format in which they could contribute it.

Elizabeth Walmsley, 2007

Conclusion:
A call to authenticity

hildren teach us about ourselves, through their presence in our lives as well as the demands they make on us. Children change us, just as the world changes us. Children open us up to love; through their beauty, their vulnerability, their honesty and the incredible love they share. Children intuitively understand the spirituality of nature through their bodies, and delight in it. Their joy is infectious and a sign of God's love.

Children remind us that God is in our bodies. They demonstrate that our flesh is not just a vessel – it is the Spirit, just as all of Nature is Spirit. When we are with children we no longer need to feel ashamed of our physical limitations. Children love us just as we are.

Children are authentic, and they call us to be authentic too.

Authenticity means that we are honest with ourselves, even when we don't like what we see. It means that we listen to our own urgings, and through quiet contemplation, discern what we are trying to tell ourselves. It means moving beyond embarrassment for the sake of saying or doing what needs to be said. It means moving beyond a fear that we are not good enough, and trusting that we will find the strength. Authenticity is about moving beyond our ego, and living in the Spirit so that we can act with love. It means standing apart from our name, our age, our educational background, our public status. It means standing as if naked, just as our children do, and being ready to take on what is asked of us.

We belong to the world. We belong to God. When we live simply, as children, then we see our true beauty in the world around us.

We are yearning for spiritual renewal. The deep crises in the world are hurting us, and we need to gather together in love. We need it, and the world needs us to get on with it.

Penn Friends Dorothy Broom and Rosie Bray at Yearly Meeting (2007)
Canberra. Photo by Tracy Bourne.

Epilogue:
A story about the future

I have a fun image in my mind.

I see a group of Quakers, standing at the edge of a canal, about to hop onto a boat. It's a wonderful sight – all ages, shapes and sizes gathered together. Everyone is laughing. They are sharing the anticipation of a journey about to begin.

They don't really know where they are heading. They have a plan, but no one has actually travelled in this direction, so they don't know what's ahead of them.

As they step on the boat, they can feel the motion of a moving surface underneath them – cradling them unsteadily. The children jostle against each other, as the adults hold their hands – trying not to lose them in the transfer from land to water.

The boat leaves the shore, and picks up speed as the pier disappears behind them. No one moves. They've put a lot of preparation into this journey, and now it has begun. The wind slaps against their bodies. Some Friends feel exposed and move deeper into the huddle of bodies. Others move to the warmth below deck. The Young Friends take control of the boat, steering it carefully through the narrow canal. The children stand at the bow, trying to see what's ahead. They lift up their faces and stick out their tongues to taste the spray.

No one speaks. They are on their way.

Appendix 1

To Friends in Amersham

FRIENDS,

Our life is love, and peace, and tenderness; and bearing one with another, and forgiving one another, and not laying accusations one against another; but praying one for another, and helping one another up with a tender hand, if there has been any slip or fall; and waiting till the Lord gives sense and repentance, if sense and repentance in any be wanting. Oh! Wait to feel this spirit, and to be guided to walk in this spirit, that ye may enjoy the Lord in sweetness, and walk sweetly, meekly, tenderly, peaceably, and lovingly one with another. And then, ye will be a praise to the Lord; and any thing that is, or hath been, or may be, amiss, ye will come over in the true dominion, even in the Lamb's dominion; and that which is contrary shall be trampled upon, as life rises and rules in you. So watch your hearts and ways; and watch one over another, in that which is gentle and tender, and knows it can neither preserve itself, nor help another out of the snare; but the Lord must be waited upon, to do this in and for us all. So mind Truth, the service, enjoyment, and possession of it in your hearts; and so to walk, as ye may bring no disgrace upon it, but may be a good saviour in the places where ye live, the meek, innocent, tender, righteous life reigning in you, governing over you, and shining through you, in the eyes of all with whom ye converse.

Your Friend in the Truth, and a desirer of your welfare and prosperity therein.
I. P.
Aylesbury, 4th of Third Month, 1667

Appendix 2

A prayer for parents

Father of us all,

We come before thee, parents and teachers of children, burdened with many concerns. We are caught in a fear that there will be no future for our children. We are beset with temptations to act in many directions at once. We would run here, run there, to prop up this corner, and then that, of our crumbling world.

Heavenly Father, what precious burden have we dropped to one side in the midst of all our frantic running? Shall we save the world and lose the soul of one untended child? Let thy light shine through our every waking moment, that we and our children may know by whom and for what we are created. Spare us from the blasphemy of taking the weight of the world upon our shoulders. Help us to lead our little ones to the true source of all being, as we have ourselves been led. And help us never to mistake action for understanding, busyness for concern, and agitation for love, lest through action, busyness and agitation we stand between our children and the living water from which they must come to drink of themselves.

Grant us the singleness of purpose to step into solitary times with our children, that thou mayest do the work in us that we cannot do of ourselves. And grant that we may together experience the outpouring of thy love, that our children may know, as we do, the one source of true joy.

We ask this in the name of one who know both love and joy, and gladly shared them with children. Amen.

By Elise Boulding
Cape May, June 1962

Appendix 3

Clothe yourself in righteousness

Adam wasn't full of knowledge,
Adam was ashamed.
Adam only knew about
that one mistake he made,

and the worst mistake ever
was to give these leaves to us.
I mean, our own doubts and fears
would be perfectly enough,

but no. We've got to hide them
and ignore what's at the roots.
We're told to love our fig leaves
more than we love the truth.

But I'm here to tell you Adam,
I'm shedding all your shame.
I'm throwing off this clothing
and I'm dancing in the rain.
I've got a lot to lose by speaking truth
but even more to gain.

So let's get naked.
Let your shame fall away
like shedding blankets.
Let your fear and your identity
hang around your ankles,

then let's run around,
show the world the stuff we've found,
the beauty we've kept hidden
underneath these
pounds and pounds
of extra clothing.

I'm shedding my self-loathing
and replacing it with trust.
I'm only here to love.
I'm through with thinking anyone's the judge.
And when we disrobe,
we let the light shine in.
We strip off the stuff that was left
from the lining.

I'm not signing autographs
'cause I don't even have a name.
I left it at the party in a pile
with all my pain.

And I'm trained to cover up.
I'm trained to hide my shame.
I'm trained in the fine art
of trying to stay sane.

In a world where judgment's passed,
where people are condemned,
we cover up our flaws long before
we work on them.

But I'm loving all my blemishes
with sentimental tenderness.
I'm writing down these sentences
defenseless.

And let's get naked.
Let your shame fall away
like shedding blankets.
Let your fear and your identity
hang around your ankles,

then let's run around,
show the world the stuff we've found,
the beauty we've kept hidden
underneath these
pounds and pounds
of extra clothing.

I'm shedding my self-loathing
and replacing it with trust.
I'm only here to love.
I'm through with thinking anyone's the
judge.

By Jon Watts
http://www.jonwatts.
com/2011/clothe-yourself-in-
righteousness-is-released/

References

1 Isaac Penington, *Letter to Amersham Friends Meeting*. 1667.

2 Kahlil Gibran, *The Prophet*. Harper Collins, 1998.

The complete phrase is: Your children are not your children. They are the sons and daughters of Life's longing for itself.

3 Helen Bayes, *Respecting the Rights of Children and Young People: A New Perspective on Quaker Faith and Practice*, The James Backhouse Lecture 2003, Australia Yearly Meeting of the Religious Society of Friends (Quakers),Melbourne, 2003.

4 Geraldine Doogue, 'Quakers: Seeking the Light Within', *Compass*, Australian Broadcasting Commission, Australia, 2003.

5 Geraldine Doogue, 'Quakers: Seeking the Light Within'.

6 Religious Society of Friends (Quakers) in Britain, *Quaker Faith and Practice*, Third edn., Yearly Meeting of the Religious Society of Friends (Quakers) in Britain, London, 2004.

7 Religious Society of Friends (Quakers) in Britain, *Quaker Faith and Practice,* Third edition, London.

8 Australia Yearly Meeting of the Religious Society of Friends (Quakers), *Handbook of Practice and Procedure in Australia*, 6th edn., Brisbane, 2011, p. 28.

9 Australia Yearly Meeting, Minutes, 1984.

10 Australia Yearly Meeting, Minutes, 1984.

11 Australia Yearly Meeting, Minute 26, 1987.

12 Australia Yearly Meeting, Minute 26, 1987.

13 Australia Yearly Meeting, Minute 28, 1988.

Penn Friends are writing 'buddies', usually between older and younger Friends, who write to each other through the year. They often catch up in person at the annual Yearly Meeting if they can.

14 Children's Committee AYM, 'Children and Quaker Meeting: Queries and Ideas', Yearly Meeting, Canberra, 1996.

15 Australia Yearly Meeting, Minute 26, 1995.

16 Australia Yearly Meeting, *Documents in Retrospect*, 1998.

17 Australia Yearly Meeting of the Religious Society of Friends (Quakers), *This we can say*, Interactive Publications, 2003, p. 110.

18 Children and Junior Young Friends Committee, Report to Australia Yearly Meeting, *Bringing Children and Junior Young Friends into the Centre of Quaker Life*, 2012.

19 Children and Junior Young Friends Committee, *Bringing Children and Junior Young Friends into the Centre of Quaker Life.*

20 Helen Bayes, *Respecting the Rights of Children and Young People*, p. 23.

21 Young Friends, *Finding our voice: Our truth, community and journey as Australian Young Friends*, The James Backhouse Lecture 2010, Australia Yearly Meeting of the Religious Society of Friends (Quakers), 2010, p. 39.

22 Young Friends, *Finding our voice: Our truth, community and journey as Australian Young Friends*, p. 55.

23 *Matthew* 18:2-3, *NIV Bible*, edn., Biblica Direct, 2012.

24 Charlie Stroud, 'Quakerism in Numerical Decline: The Way Forward', *An essay submitted for the 2009 Prize Essay Competition: 'The Future of the Religious Society of Friends in Britain'*, Britain Yearly Meeting, London, 2009.

25 Children and Junior Young Friends Committee, Report to Australia Yearly Meeting Standing Committee, 2009

26 Matthew 18:2-3

27 From the *Beatitudes, Matthew* 5:3-10, *NIV Bible*, edn., Biblica Direct, 2012.

28 Lynda Payne, 'Health in England (16th–18th c.)', in *Children and Youth in History*, Accessed 21 May, 2013. <http://chnm.gmu.edu/cyh/teaching-modules/166>

29 Helen Bayes, *Respecting the Rights of Children and Young People*, p. 43.

30 Helen Bayes, 'In Respect of Children: Another look at Equality and Non-violence in Quaker Practice', *Woodbrooke Lecture Series: A Century of Quaker Witness*, Religious Society of Friends, Woodbrooke, 2003.

31 Lucy Violet Hodgkin, *A Book of Quaker Saints*, Macmillan and Co, London, 1922.

32 George Fox, *George Fox: An Autobiography*, ed. Rufus Jones, Christian Classics Ethereal Library, <http://www.ccel.org/ccel/fox_g/autobio.titlepage.html>1908, p. 8.

33 George Fox, *George Fox: An Autobiography*, p.29-30

34 Barbara Luetke-Stahlman, *17th Century Remarkable Quaker Youth*, Sir Speedy Printing, Olanthe, KS, 2001.

35 Phyllis Mack, *Visionary Women: Ecstatic Prophecy in Seventeenth-Century England*, University of California Press, Berkeley, 1992.

36 Barbara Luetke-Stahlman, *17th Century Remarkable Quaker Youth.*

37 Lucy Violet Hodgkin, *A Book of Quaker Saints.*

38 J. Sowle, *An Abstract of the Sufferings of the People called Quakers*, Vol. 1: 1650-1660, Sowle, London. Original publication by Oxford University Press, 1733. Digitised in 2008 by Google Books, p. 200.

39 J. Sowle, *An Abstract of the Sufferings of the People called Quakers*, p. 201.

40 Kirstin Olsen, *Chronology of Women's History*, Greenwood Press, Westport, 1994.

41 Christine Trevett, *Women and Quakerism in the 17th Century*, The Ebor Press, York, 1991.

42 Jon Watts, Accessed 7 June 2013, <http://www.jonwatts.com/2011/clothe-yourself-in-righteousness-is-released/>

43 Magdalene Harrison, 'Clothe Yourself in Righteousness: But First Get Naked!', Self Published, http://www.ClotheYourselfinRighteousness.com, 2012.

44 Harold Loukes, *Friends and their Children: A Study in Quaker Education*, George G. Harrap & Co. Ltd, London, 1958.

45 Phyllis Mack, *Visionary Women: Ecstatic Prophecy in Seventeenth-Century England*, p. 211.

46 Mary Sherlock, *Living Simply with Children: a voluntary simplicity guide for moms, dads, and kids who want to reclaim the bliss of childhood and the joy of parenting*, Three Rivers Press, New York, 2003.

47 Hugh Mackay, *The Good Life: What Makes a Life Worth Living?*, Pan MacMillan Australia, Sydney, 2013, p. 16.

48 Clive Hamilton & Richard Denniss, *Affluenza: When Too Much is Never Enough*, Allen and Unwin, Crows Nest, NSW, 2005.

49 Clive Hamilton & Richard Denniss, *Affluenza: When Too Much is Never Enough*.

50 Hugh Mackay, *The Good Life: What Makes a Life Worth Living?*

51 Hugh Mackay, *The Good Life: What Makes a Life Worth Living?*

52 Fiona Stanley, Sue Richardson & Margot Prior, *Children of the Lucky Country?: How Australian Society has turned its back on children and why children matter*, Pan Macmillan Australia, Sydney, 2005.

53 Fiona Stanley, Sue Richardson & Margot Prior, *Children of the Lucky Country?*

54 Fiona Stanley, Sue Richardson & Margot Prior, *Children of the Lucky Country?*

55 Australian Bureau of Statistics, 'Children's Participation in Cultural and Leisure Activities, Australia, 2011-12', Accessed 14 August 2013, <http://www.abs.gov.au/ausstats/abs@.nsf/Latestproducts/4901.0Main%20Features6Apr%202012?opendocument&tabname=Summary&prodno=4901.0&issue=Apr%202012&num=&view= >

56 Fiona Stanley, Sue Richardson & Margot Prior, *Children of the Lucky Country?*

57 Richard Louv, *Last Child in the Woods: Saving Our Children from Nature-Deficit Disorder*, Atlantic Books, London, 2005.

58 Stephen Zubrick et. al., 'Nothing But Fear Itself: Parental fear as a determinant impacting on child physical activity and independant mobility', in *Victorian Health Promotion Foundation (VicHealth) (ed)*, Accessed 14 August 2013, http://www.vichealth.vic.gov.au/Publications/Physical-Activity/Active-transport/Nothing-But-Fear-Itself.aspx, Melbourne, 2010.

59 Stephen Zubrick et. al., 'Nothing But Fear Itself: Parental fear as a determinant impacting on child physical activity and independant mobility', p. 291-306.

60 Jon Watts, 'Why High School Sucked: and how Young Friends Saved My Life', *Friends Journal: Quaker Thought and Life Today*, vol. July 2007, p. 33-5.

61 Quoted in Lucy Violet Hodgkin, *A Book of Quaker Saints*, Kindle location 2906.

62 James Fowler, *Stages of Faith: The Psychology of Human Development and the Quest for Meaning*, Harper Collins, San Francisco, 1995.

63 David Hay & Rebecca Nye, *The Spirit of the Child*, Jessica Kingsley Publishers, London, 1998.

64 Vivienne Mountain, 'Investigating the meaning and function of prayer for children in selected primary schools in Melbourne Australia', PhD, Australian Catholic University, 2004.

65 2 *Corinthians* 3:6. *NIV Bible*, edn., Biblica Direct, 2012.

The full text is: *He has made us competent as ministers of a new covenant—not of the letter but of the Spirit; for the letter kills, but the Spirit gives life.*

66 Helen Bayes in Australia Yearly Meeting of the Religious Society of Friends (Quakers), *This We Can Say*, p. 202.

67 Francisco Gonzales in Australian Young Friends Book Committee (ed), *Footprints and Echoes*, Young Friends, Australia Yearly Meeting of the Religious Society of Friends (Quakers), 2008.

68 Sandy Parker in Australia Yearly Meeting of the Religious Society of Friends (Quakers), *This We Can Say*, p. 244.

69 Howard Nurden & Simon Best, 'A theological basis for children and young people's participation in Quaker decision-making', in Britain Yearly Meeting (ed), <http://www.quaker.org.uk/participation-policy>, 2006.

70 Isaac Penington in Australia Yearly Meeting of the Religious Society of Friends (Quakers), *This We Can Say*, p. 242.

71 Elizabeth Walmsley, 'How Monthly Meetings Can Support Their Youth', *Friends Journal: Quaker Thought and Life Today*, July 2007.